WIND POWER

Nicolas Brasch

Rigby

www.Rigby.com
1-800-531-5015

Rigby Focus Forward

Published in 2007 by Nelson Australia Pty Ltd ACN: 058 280 149
A Cengage Learning company

1 2 3 4 5 6 7 8 374 14 13 12 11 10 09 08 07
Printed and bound in China

Wind Power
ISBN-13   978-1-4190-3811-2
ISBN-10   1-4190-3811-7

Acknowledgments
The author and publisher would like to acknowledge permission to reproduce material
from the following sources:
Photographs by Fotolia/ Broker, front cover bottom, front cover left, pp. 14 top, 23 left/
Jostein Hauge, p. 11; Istockphoto, p. 8 left/ Guillermo Perales Gonzalez, p. 16 top/ Rafa
Irusta, p. 9/ Stephen Hoerold, p. 19; Lindsay Edwards, back cover, front cover right, pp.
5, 6-7, 8 right, 10 left, 13 left, 15 left, 16 bottom, 17 right, 18 right, 21 left, 22 left, 23
right; Masterfile, p. 12/ Bill Brooks, p. 22 right; Photolibrary/ Alamy/ Directphoto.org, p.
14 bottom/ Darrell Gulin, p. 18 left/ Hank Delespinasse, p. 21 right/ IFA – Bilderteam
Gmbh, p. 10 right/ Photo Researchers, p. 13 right/ Richard Cummins, front cover top, p.
20/ Robin Smith, pp. 15 right, 17 top.

WIND POWER

Nicolas Brasch

Contents

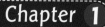

Chapter 1

THE COMMUNITY MEETING

Welcome to the Gale Hills Town Hall
for tonight's special community meeting.

My name is Sarah Wattle,
and I'm the mayor of Gale Hills.

The issue for discussion tonight
is wind power.

This is a very important issue for our town—
a company called Wind Future
wants to erect wind **turbines** in Gale Hills.

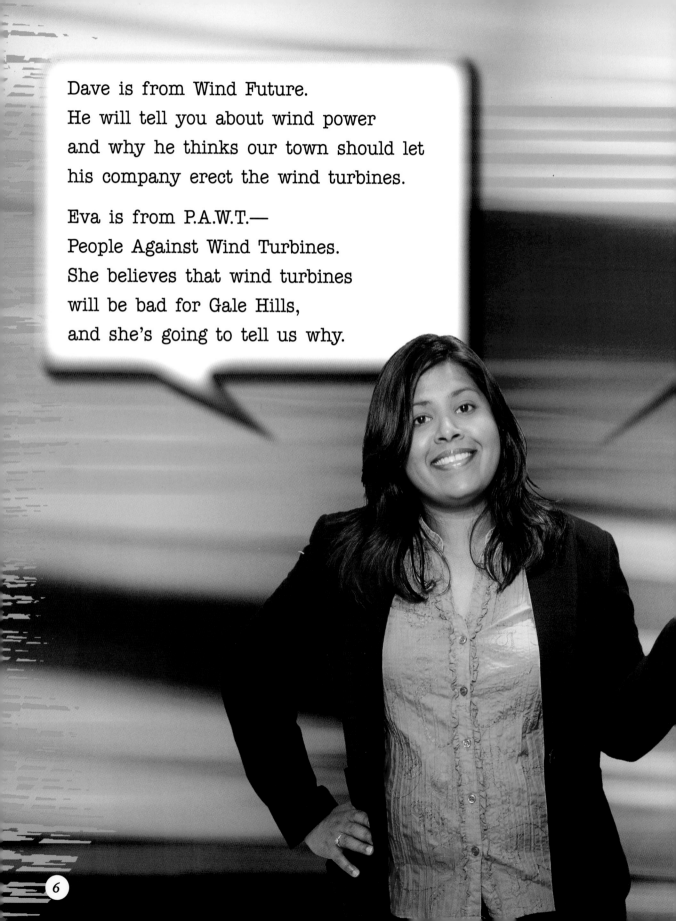

Dave is from Wind Future.
He will tell you about wind power
and why he thinks our town should let
his company erect the wind turbines.

Eva is from P.A.W.T.—
People Against Wind Turbines.
She believes that wind turbines
will be bad for Gale Hills,
and she's going to tell us why.

After they have both presented
their points of view,
we should be in a better position
to decide what we want for Gale Hills.

Now please welcome Dave to the stage!

Chapter 2

THE CASE FOR WIND POWER

Thank you, Sarah.
It's great to be here.
I love Gale Hills.

One reason I love this town so much is because it's perfect for wind power.

Wind power is created by wind turbines.

The blades of the turbine are powered
by the wind, and when the blades turn,
they power a **generator** that is inside the turbine.
This generator creates electricity.

There are more than 85,000 wind turbines
around the world.
I believe it's about time that Gale Hills had some.

a coal mine

Wind power is a clean form of **energy**.
The more wind power we use,
the less we need to use other energy sources,
like coal.

a power plant

Using coal to produce electricity
creates a lot of **greenhouse gases**.

Greenhouse gases harm the environment
and may be responsible for rising temperatures
around the world.
If temperatures keep rising,
many animal species will become **extinct**.

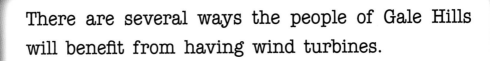

There are several ways the people of Gale Hills will benefit from having wind turbines.

First, we will pay the people who agree to have a wind turbine on their property.

Most of these people will be farmers.

A wind turbine guarantees the property owners money each year, something which isn't guaranteed by planting crops.

Second, the wind turbines will attract tourists to the town.
There are no other wind turbines near here, and people will be interested in seeing them.

Third, you will have access to the electricity generated by the wind turbines.

It's possible to build a wind turbine
that will provide all the electricity needed
by more than 700 households.

So I say to you, please agree to have wind turbines in Gale Hills.
You will all benefit!

THE CASE AGAINST WIND POWER

Thank you, Mayor Wattle.

I'm against wind turbines in Gale Hills
for three main reasons.

First, they destroy the landscape.
We have a beautiful landscape with unspoiled hills.
We do not want wind turbines
spoiling the view.

When you look out of your window in the morning, do you want to see rolling hills and running streams? Or do you want to see wind turbine blades spinning around?

Second, wind turbines are noisy.
The windier it is, the noisier they are.
Wind Future says that Gale Hills
is a great choice for wind turbines
because of the amount of wind
we have.

That means the wind turbines
are going to be very, very noisy.

Third, birds and bats might fly into the blades
and be killed.

We have many species of birds around Gale Hills,
as well as a bat colony,
and we don't want to put these creatures
in danger.

So I say to you all tonight—
please don't let wind turbines be built in Gale Hills.

Chapter 4

THINK LONG AND HARD

Thank you, Eva, and thank you again, Dave. That was a very interesting discussion.

When the time comes for you all to vote on whether we should have wind turbines in Gale Hills, you will be well informed.

I ask you to think long and hard about this issue.

Glossary

energy   power

extinct   no longer in existence

generator   a machine that creates power

greenhouse gases   gases that contribute to the greenhouse effect

turbines   a revolving machine that produces continuous power by the fast-moving flow of air

Index